**Philippine Copyright © 2020
by Rowena Bernal**

All rights reserved. No part of this publication may be reproduced, distributed, or transmitted in any form or by any means, including photocopying, recording, or other electronic or mechanical methods, without the prior written permission of the author, except in the case of brief quotations embodied in critical reviews and certain other noncommercial uses permitted by copyright law. For permission queries, you may write to the author at the email address
rowena.bernal2015@gmail.com.

2ⁿᵈ Edition

Published by: Alphabet House

ISBN: 978-621-96335-0-5

My ABCD of
I Know Me

Table of Content

Acknowledgement and Notes ………….. 4
Dedication ………….. 5
Introduction ………….. 7
Letters of the Alphabet
    A ………….. 8
    B ………….. 10
    C ………….. 14
    D ………….. 16
    E ………….. 18
    F ………….. 20
    G ………….. 22
    H ………….. 24
    I ………….. 26
    J ………….. 28
    K ………….. 30
    L ………….. 32
    M ………….. 36
    N ………….. 38
    O ………….. 40
    P ………….. 42
    Q ………….. 46
    R ………….. 48
    S ………….. 50
    T ………….. 52
    U ………….. 54
    V ………….. 56
    W ………….. 58
    X ………….. 60
    Y ………….. 62
    Z ………….. 64
My Own Version of ABCD ………….. 66
Epilogue …………...70

Acknowledgement and Notes

A special thanks goes out to **Cecille Orquiola** for her incredible creativity and attention to detail in designing my book cover and pages.

The drawing on page 38 was drawn by **Brandon Bernal** when he was four years old.

The photo on page 36 was taken by **Joyce Bernal**.

The cover photo and all the photos representing the letters were taken in the Philippines and are properties of the author.

The author greatly appreciates the loving support of her family – **Nanay, Ena** and **Alvin, Lyn** and **Reggie, Ambet, Engkay, Ingkis** – and **in-laws**, all of whom provided refuge when she needed it most.

Dondon (+), Brandon and **Jakob** are the author's main source of strength and inspiration.

Hi!

I would like

to let you know -

To you who struggles;

To you who have loved and lost;

To you who feels life has been unkind;

To you who look forward to happy thoughts;

To you who has just sent a prayer to heaven;

To you who keeps greeting each day with a smile;

To you who have been looking for a push to keep you going;

To you who work every day so you could provide for your family;

To you who finds happiness in leafing through the pages of a book;

This book is for YOU.

_____

I would love to hear what you think. You can visit my blog or FB page and get in touch.

Blog: https://reflections-mylifeinwords.blogspot.com/

FB page: https://www.facebook.com/reflections.mylifeinwords

Introduction

You know, they say you learn all the things that you need from childhood to adulthood in Kindergarten. With that in mind, let us see if the basic alphabet is still true as you become older. And yes, we can still sing ABCD with all our heart but this time, it will not be "a is for apple" nor "b is for ball." You see, you get to know yourself with this new ABCD.

As you read through each letter, I hope you will find life a little bit easier, and this world a little bit friendlier. Life is full of unexpected gifts and it is an unfathomable well of pleasant and unpleasant surprises. It comes with intertwined emotions - happiness, frustration, exultation, fear, courage, grief, pain, and a myriad other. As we grow older, we encounter more and more of these surprises and emotions. Sometimes they bring us the greatest joys; sometimes they bring us unimaginable sadness, but they are all part of our beautiful journey.

Happy reading!

ALLOW YOURSELF TO GROW

Like everything else in life, this must start with YOU because you are your best shot. Imagine yourself standing on the beach, staring at the orange rays of the sunset, thinking about the day. Ask yourself, have I been nice to my self today? Have I given myself the opportunity to improve and to grow? Did I nurture myself? Reflect on your answers and feel the calm that comes with understanding how you deal with yourself.

You are your best cheerleader. When your shoulders feel heavy from burden and pain, be the first to tell yourself that you can do it. When you think you cannot continue anymore, be the first to remind yourself that you can still take one small step at a time. When you cannot see what your life is all about, look in the mirror, and remind yourself, "you are beautiful, you are worthy, you are a work in progress."

Be aware of what you can do and what you can further improve on. Know yourself, your gifts, and your talents. Participate in activities that enhance your talents. You've got to set aside time and

effort to nurture yourself. It is about finding the time to know yourself, your needs, and how to make yourself better. Living life to the fullest starts with knowing what you can do best and where you can step back. When you know this much about yourself, you are in the best position to help yourself grow and become better and happier.

This is your space. Think about the areas in your life that are ready for growth. What can you do to help yourself?

SELF CARE

_____
_____
_____
_____
_____
_____
_____

FAMILY

_____
_____
_____
_____
_____
_____
_____

SOCIAL

_____
_____
_____
_____
_____
_____
_____

PROFESSIONAL

_____
_____
_____
_____
_____
_____
_____

BE HERE NOW

I like thinking about the past and planning for the future until one day I realized there is a missing link – the present. It is good to remember the past and plan for the future, but hey, we live in the NOW, in the present, so you have to be right here, right now.

Live this day. Being here now can pertain to a lot of things - being here now to address your state of health; being here now to start all those things that you have planned; being here now to love the people around you; being here now to recognize and enjoy what you have. The past is a source of good memories and inspiration, but we cannot spend our lifetime just reliving those memories. The future is a source of hope and tomorrow is something to look forward to, but we have to make sure that we do not spend most of our time daydreaming about what the future will be, and in the process taking for granted what we have in our lives today. We have the present to love and live.

Take a deep breath. Smile while remembering your past, be positive while you hope for a better future, and focus on now.

Celebrate what you have today!

Think about your relationships — with your self, family and friends. Where are they right now?

Family

Remember-ing the past	On the way to the present	Enjoying the present	Torn between present and future	Fixed on the future

Friends

Remember-ing the past	On the way to the present	Enjoying the present	Torn between present and future	Fixed on the future

Self

Remember-ing the past	On the way to the present	Enjoying the present	Torn between present and future	Fixed on the future

What are you going to do to be here — in the present?

Name the people, things, and events that you are leaving behind in the past.

Your priorities for the present:

_____ :
_____
_____
_____ :
_____
_____
_____ :
_____
_____
_____ :
_____
_____

CHANGE IS INEVITABLE; BE READY FOR IT

I like looking at old photo albums because no matter how many times you look at the old photos, you will still be surprised at how much things have changed. You often ask, "is this really me?" Or you look at another family member and say, "I can't believe this is you." As years go by, we change. People around us change. Our circumstances change.

The world is changing, and we cannot stop it. All we can do is to be the best we can be as we navigate the changes around us and within us. We can like or dislike the changes but there is no stopping these changes. We do not have control over what will happen next or what will change next, but we can turn our experiences into something positive and useful for us. We have to learn how to adapt and change. Expect change to come like an uninvited visitor. When the change is painful and frustrating or when you are at the darkest bottom of life, remember the old Persian saying, "This too shall pass."

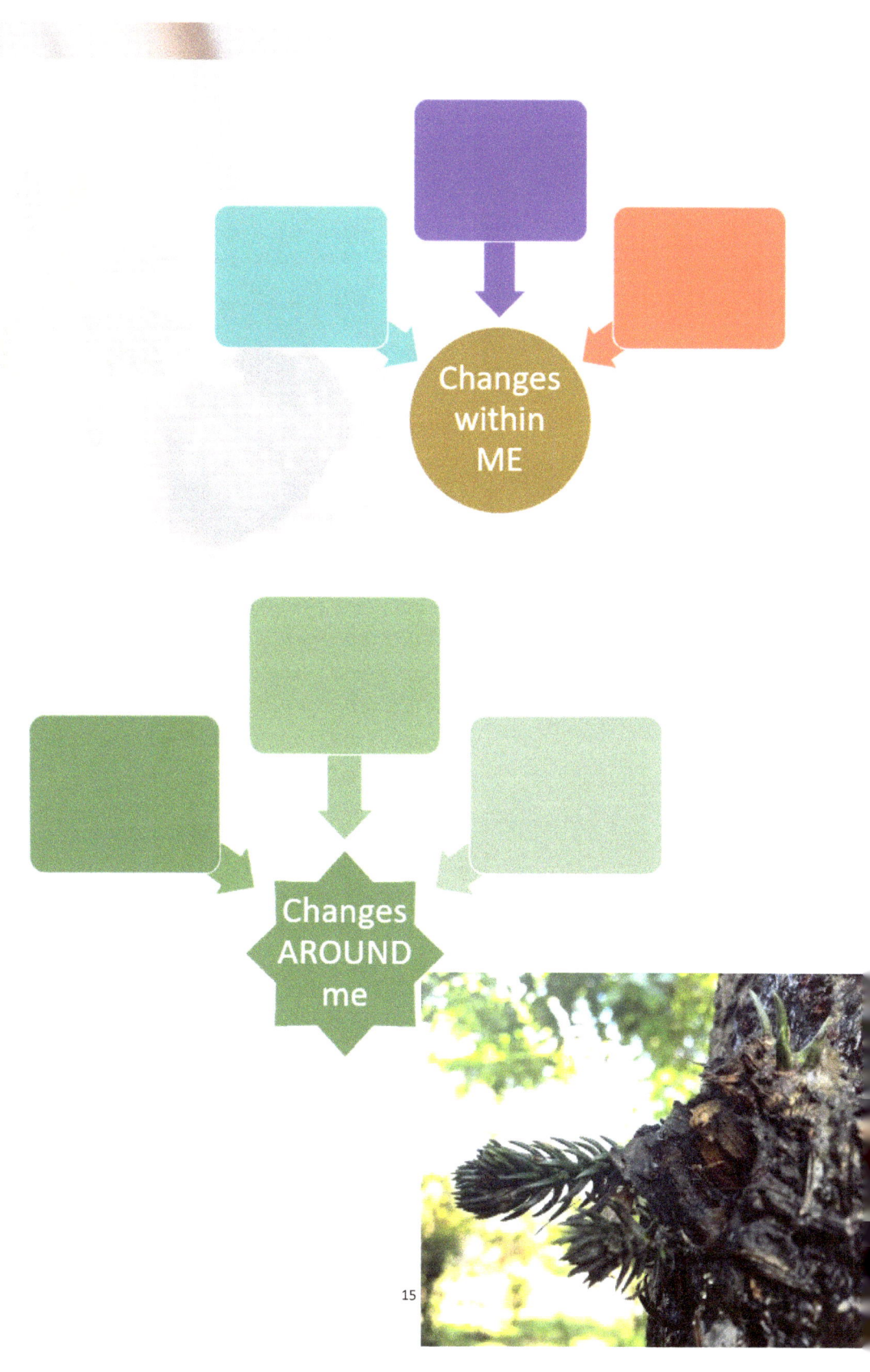

DARE TO KEEP ON DREAMING

When I was a university student, I read in a marketing brochure that Walt Disney was the biggest dreamer of all. From a drawing of a mouse he built a name and an empire that children of various generations all over the world have come to know and love. Dreams are very powerful, and they are free. It is a cliché when people say, "never stop dreaming." But what else can you say? Without dreams, what is there to look forward to? Dreams do not always have to be that of grandeur, power, fame, and riches. Dreams can be simple and very personal. A great dream is anything that can make you happy and fulfilled.

Now and then, things happen, and the dreams that we have been building, the things that we have been planning, will not happen. In that event, we should have the strength and the courage to keep on dreaming.

I think "dare to dream" is easier to think of when you are younger, say in your 20s. But when you reach your 40s, the saying 'dare to dream' is met with smirk. "At my age?" they'll say. Yes!!!! Keep on dreaming because we must. When we stop dreaming, then we stop living. When we stop dreaming, there is a part of us that stops growing, there is a part of us that stops talking, there is a part of us that stops looking for what else we can do, and there is a part in our heart that stops beating.

We owe it to ourselves to keep on dreaming. Dreaming is not just about wanting something in the future, it is also about us believing that things will be better, it is us believing that we can make other lives better. It is us believing that we can.

> **Draw a SYMBOL of your dream here. Every time things get difficult, look at this symbol and be reminded of your dream.**

EXPRESS YOUR HAPPINESS

Do you remember the nursery rhyme, "When you're happy and you know it, clap your hands…?" When you are happy, and you know you are happy, show the world that you are. Happiness begets happiness so show it and it will be a magnet that will attract more happiness. Ask yourself, when was the world at its most beautiful? When was life at its brightest? I can bet that your answer was "when I was happy." Isn't Aristotle, the great philosopher, right when he said that the ultimate goal of every human being is happiness? Think of any accomplished man or woman and think of the poorest of the poor. They all have the same goal – to be happy.

Let yourself feel the happiness that comes from small things around you and foster happy memories – seeing the rainbow, watching the flower bloom, witnessing a child walk for the first time, listening to birds chirping in the morning, enjoying the smell of the newly cut grass. The happiness that comes from these activities will build up and give you a sort of happiness reserve that you can withdraw from when life is not being kind. Small things, big things, simple things, grand things - celebrate every single thing that makes you happy.

Happiness is...

Food that makes you happy	Thoughts that make you happy
People that make you happy	Memories that make you happy

Recall your happy story here

_____
_____
_____
_____
_____
_____
_____
_____
_____
_____
_____
_____
_____
_____

FOREVER HAVE FAITH

Where would I be if I did not have faith? I am sure I would be nowhere. I would be lost without faith because faith is my anchor and my guide. Faith is that feeling that clings to your heart and tells you that you are never alone, even if circumstances and the people around you make you feel otherwise. It is a powerful tonic that keeps you holding on even though the rope is as thin as thread. When you are down and the world is dark, it is that invisible hand that lifts you up and gives you light.

Having gone through so much in my life, I am a living testament to how far faith can keep you going. There was a time in my life when I was a refugee because of a volcanic eruption and my family did not have anything to eat on most days, no clothes except for what we were wearing, no place to stay in, nor money for our needs. All we had was our faith in God. Every day, I recited, in my mind, the passage from the bible, "He who had given us his only son, how can he not also, along with him, graciously give us all things?" And that was enough for me to believe that God will answer my prayers. My rumbling stomach was calmed by repeatedly reading the verse from Matthew 6:25 – *Therefore, I say to you, do not worry about your life, what you will eat or what you will drink; nor about your body, what you will put on. Is not life more than food, and the body more than clothing?*

Have faith in the supreme being that you believe in. Have faith in the people around you. Have faith in the goodness of this world. Have faith in the positive energies that revolve around you. Have faith in your vision. Have faith in your destiny.

I have faith in _____

because _____

_____

_____

_____

_____

_____

GET ONE AND PASS

When I was in grade school and something was being distributed to the class, the teacher would say "*get one and pass*" to make sure each one gets his/her share. This is a thought that we should consider in our everyday lives too. Our desire to reach our ambitions should be tempered by our thoughts of others. When we are too focused on achieving our goals, there is a risk of being too consumed with those goals and set aside the need of others. This makes us overlook the fact that we should leave something for other people and leave time for other important things. Taking into consideration the needs of others should soften our actions in wanting to get more or do more. Think of moderation – anything in excess is never good, so take what we need and leave something for others.

The Covid-19 pandemic has reminded us of many basic things that we take for granted, including how we react when we know that there might not be enough for everyone. We have seen videos and heard news about hoarding, about people wanting all for themselves, leaving others with nothing. In our everyday lives, in our personal and professional lives, we should always remember that we live in a community, and that we are part of a greater community. Just get one and pass the rest to others, whatever the

thing or opportunity may be. This is a reminder for us that while we work our way to the top, we should see to it that we are not taking from others nor depriving them of the opportunity. This is true whether you are a follower or a leader. When confronted with a situation that makes you ask yourself, *do I have enough* or *am I taking away from others*, listen to your heart and understand when it says, just get one and pass.

What I need

What I have in abundance that I can share

HOLD ON TO HOPE AT ALL TIMES

Hope is that untouchable certainty in your heart and in your head that things will be better. Hope makes you continue to look forward to tomorrow because you strongly believe that there is something good waiting for you. You believe that whatever unhappy circumstances you are in will end and the new day will start bright.

What makes you want to wake up in the morning even though the previous day/night has sucked your energy dry as you try to survive? What makes you successfully go through another horrible day? What makes you smile after an unspeakable heartbreak? What makes you keep on trying even when you know you might fall again? What is that feeling that pushes you to keep going when your limbs can barely carry you? That, my friend, is hope. It will never give up on you - when things are bad, we can continue to soldier on because there is hope that it will be better. When people's feelings are hurt, we can move on because we hope that there will be forgiveness. We hope that with every sunrise comes a better day and a new beginning. We hope that with every sunset, we are closing a chapter to start a beautiful new one.

Life is a gift because there is hope. Unwrap it with a smile, a prayer, and a lot of hope.

Recall the times when HOPE carried you through difficult times. Write them below.

INSPIRE AND BE INSPIRED

When I was a teenager, I enjoyed reading how great men and women once dreamed of what they wanted in life, worked hard for it, never compromised their dream and eventually achieved what they wanted. I went to sleep at night thinking about how Mother Theresa, Hellen Keller, and Marie Curie persevered, never gave up, and never stopped fighting for their beliefs and dreams against all odds. It gave me strength reading their stories. And then of course, we have Bill Gates and Steve Jobs who revolutionized our way of life. I am inspired by their lives, by their achievements, by their beliefs, and by their ideas. I listened over and over again to Steve Jobs' speech as a commencement speaker in a prestigious university because it made my heart swell with inspiration and determination to keep going. I kept repeating his closing line – stay foolish, stay hungry - and it kept me inspired.

You have to work with people and ideas that inspire you. Surround yourself with people that have the zest and determination to make life better for others. I have a friend who was a teacher in a Multigrade school. She was so dedicated to her students that she saw every single day as an opportunity to support students. Her school did not have a library, so she built a library on a tree and had a library tree house. The books in her library were amazing. You know why? They were actively used by the students. Students laughed and played and read! Looking back at what she did and listening to her talk was truly inspirational. It made me think back to what I want, my advocacies and my desire to help others. People who give more than what is required of them are a great source of inspiration. In the same manner, make it a part of your habit to inspire others. Giving your best shot in everything that you do, taking care of the people you work with, and working towards the greater good will inspire the people in your team to be the best that they can be. Let your work and your relationship with others be a source of inspiration for the people around you.

Fill the screen with the most inspirational quote you have ever read or heard.

JUST SAY GOODBYE ANY TIME YOU NEED TO

Shake it off my friend. Dust it off your heart. If it does not have a place in your life, cough it out of your system. There are things, habits, places, feelings, thoughts, memories and people that you feel like you need to say goodbye to but find it very difficult to do so, and it is making you feel weak and tired. You are wasting time and effort thinking about it. It is ruining your good mood and making your day difficult. Then, there's the anger that had been eating at your heart for some time now. There's a grudge, an affronted feeling that you're still holding on to. What should you do? Let go. If it is time to say goodbye, if it is time to let go, then, just let go. There is nothing else that will make things better except to let go. Yes, it is difficult, even painful, but it is something that you must do. Find your courage and say goodbye.

One of the most difficult things that I have done was to let go of pain and anger. When I was not allowing myself to let go, I was consumed by negative energies and thoughts, especially when faced with a difficult situation, which in turn fed jealousy, animosity, hopelessness and hate. It was debilitating and nothing could make me happy. So, I did what I had to do – let go. And when I made that decision, I was deliriously happy. I was free at last!

We do what we have to do – let go, now! You are brave and powerful. You have the courage and the power to let go. Use your power!

Close your eyes. Think of what you would like to say goodbye to. Imagine yourself releasing it, and seeing it disappear in the horizon. Draw an image that you will think of when you want to let go of something or someone.

KEEP THE FIRE BURNING

When we are fighting for anything, whether it is a dream, an advocacy, a belief, or a goal, there will be bumps along the way that will serve as pauses and stops. To keep on going despite these bumps, we must continue to feed the fire of passion within us.

It is easy to be ecstatic and inspired when you can easily envision the impact of what you are doing, when you can see results, or when it is clear where you are going. However, it is so much more difficult to continue when you are in a plateau. When things look boring, how do you stay interested? When things do not seem to be moving, how do you stay passionate? When your personal circumstances make you feel nothing else but pain, how much more will you be willing to take before you give up? How do you stay interested, focused, and in the fight when you are in despair? You must have the grit to keep your fire of passion and determination burning.

When I was growing up as a teenager, we were living in a small hut with used cement sacks for walls and coconut leaves for roof. There was barely food on the table, and yet in my mind and in my heart, there was no space for giving up. There was just the intention to survive, move forward and fight for a better life. I welcomed the hunger, the

pain, and the humiliation because it was part of the fight. When I feel tired and almost extinguished, I push myself to think of things that will keep my fire burning.

These are my strategies to keep my fire burning:

LOVE FOR AS LONG AS YOU LIVE

Growing up, my consciousness is filled with clichés such as "love conquers all," and "love makes the world go round." In school and community bible studies, we talked about God's unconditional love and family love. At a very young age, we were assured by our family that we are loved. We share love with our friends. We are encouraged to love our neighbors and help them in times of need. We all know that we cannot live in a world without love.

Love is so powerful that it makes things that look impossible become possible. It allows you to give more when you thought there was nothing more to give. Here, I would like to focus on the love that we all need; the kind of love that transforms you into a caring, empathetic human being. You look at your children, your parents, your siblings, your friends; it is so easy to love the people that we care about. It is so easy to share the happy feelings with them. But the love that will make this world a better place for everyone is the love that transcends blood relations and does not expect anything in return; a love that transcends hatred

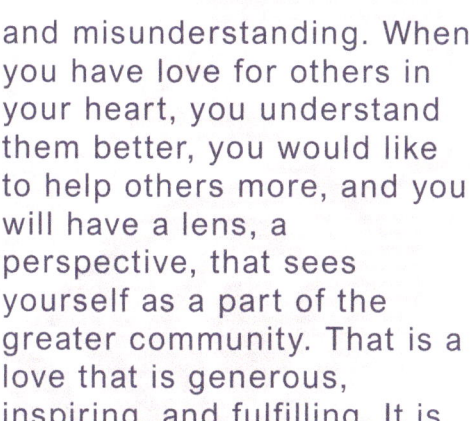

and misunderstanding. When you have love for others in your heart, you understand them better, you would like to help others more, and you will have a lens, a perspective, that sees yourself as a part of the greater community. That is a love that is generous, inspiring, and fulfilling. It is the kind of love that will truly make this world go round.

We have to be careful though. Sometimes, because we love, we are also more vulnerable to pain and disappointment. We see the suffering in this world, and we wonder if people still feel love. We see greed and betrayal on monumental scales, and we wonder, how can they not love their neighbor. We see hunger and death and we wonder, where is love? There are times when we would think it would be better to just not care, to just not love, because that will free us from feeling the agony that others feel, but we should never give in to this temptation. Letting go of love in our hearts because we do not want to witness and feel the suffering of others will make the suffering worse for others. It will create a bigger circle of apathy, which in the end will contribute to more sorrow for others.

We have to be steadfast in our love. Let it reside in the safest place in our heart and let it be our refuge when we are not sure how to continue with our journey in this world.

Three words I associate with LOVE:

Write inside each heart a name you associate with love:

My own quote about love:

"_____

_____

_____

_____

_____

                                                                    "
_____

My greatest story of LOVE

MOVE MOUNTAINS, BUT ONLY WHEN YOU NEED TO

To achieve what we want and to reach our dreams, we must be prepared to move mountains but ... only when we need to. Let us be smart in making decisions and choosing our battles. It is very important to fully understand ourselves, our goals and our circumstances so that we will not get too focused on the mountain in front of us that can unnecessarily use up all our time and resources; only to realize later on that we did not have to move the mountain at all. Any time there is a mountain that blocks the view of where we want to go or cuts the path to where we should be, let us start by asking ourselves: Do I need to move the mountain or can I just hike through it, or walk around it?

What will it take to move the mountain? By moving the mountain, will things get better or worse? Energy is created as well as spent. For every battle in life we spend our energy. Spend your energy wisely. You do not have to be standing ready with your sword at every point. Choose your fights. Choose the ones that will have an impact in your life.

If your core values will not be compromised, and you can still accomplish what

you want to do by walking around the mountain or through it, then, you do not have to move the mountain. In addition to making life easier, you are also conserving your energy and resources so that by the time a mountain that should really be moved shows up, you will still have the strength and the capability to move that mountain.

Challenge: _____

Do you need to move the mountain?

NO — What will you do instead?

_____
_____
_____
_____
_____
_____

YES — What do you need to successfully move the mountain?

_____
_____
_____
_____
_____
_____

NEVER LOSE SIGHT OF WHAT MATTERS

When you were faced with something as powerful as the Covid-19 pandemic, what was the most important thing on your mind? I am pretty sure going home and staying safe were on top of your list. That flight that you had to take? It did not take off. The project that you will start? It did not happen. That comfort food you cannot live without? You can actually survive without it.

The covid-19 pandemic has shown us that no matter how much we thought things were indispensable, or how missing a deadline or a meeting is just not possible, things can and will stop. In the face of this threat, nothing was important but the most basic of all – family and health. Everything else took a backseat.

So, when we go to work or when we go out to attend meetings or buy things and properties, remember that these are not our priorities. Reflect on what matters most to you. When you know that

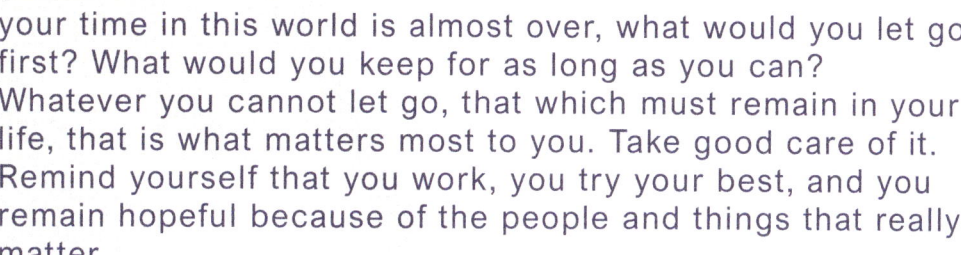

your time in this world is almost over, what would you let go first? What would you keep for as long as you can? Whatever you cannot let go, that which must remain in your life, that is what matters most to you. Take good care of it. Remind yourself that you work, you try your best, and you remain hopeful because of the people and things that really matter.

Draw what matters most to you.

OPEN YOUR HEART TO OTHERS

My husband stayed in the ICU for 3 days, and when on the 3rd day he left this world, I was left crying in the middle of a void, an empty place where there was nothing – no faces, no sound, no awareness of time. It was just me, the tears and the unbearable pain. And when my strength left, I fell. But halfway to my fall, someone caught me – a companion of another patient. I don't remember anything about this person but the kindness and comfort this person provided me at my darkest moment remains vivid in my memory. On this stranger's shoulder I wept for several minutes until I regained my ability to feel and think. At that moment that person was my angel.

When you can be another person's angel, open your heart and take on the role. This world needs more people who are willing to be there for others without expecting anything. Offer kind words when you know that the other person needs it. One word of encouragement can make a difference in another

person's life. Be deliberate in your willingness to embrace and help someone who needs help, no matter how you feel about the person or the circumstances this person may be in. When you see another person going through difficult times, do the extra mile of reaching out and letting the other person know that there is someone in this world who cares.

Think of *three good deeds* that you will do, moving forward, without expecting appreciation or anything in return.

Good deed #1

For whom: _____

What will it be:

_____
_____
_____
_____
_____

Good deed #2

For whom: _____

What will it be:

_____
_____
_____
_____
_____

Good deed #3

For whom: _____

What will it be:

_____
_____
_____
_____
_____

PRAY, BECAUSE GOD IS LISTENING

Life happens, and with it are the trials, heartbreaks and buckets of tears but if we have our faith, and we have it strong, we will never lose our way. To stay on track, we just have to
believe in every word that God has given us in the Bible.

I grew up in poverty, but God never failed to
provide help when we need it most. Despite not having material things, despite going hungry on most days, I never felt despair because I knew that there was God. I've had many triumphs in this backdrop of poverty because I believed in God.

When I am weary or I feel internal turmoil or I want something so bad, I stop, bend my knees and pray, comforted by the belief in the words I first heard when I was a college freshman student - *anything you ask for in prayer, believe that you have received it, and it will be yours*. Then, I repeat in my mind over and over again, "*He who had given us*

his only son, how can he not, along with him, graciously give us all things." Then, my heart will be peaceful, and indeed I got the things that I prayed for.

However, when our life does not seem to go with what we want no matter how much we believe in God, we feel frustrated. There are times when we feel that God has somehow turned his back on us; that somehow, he can hear us but decided to ignore us, and this is the most difficult dark hole to crawl out of. When this happens, give yourself some space. Even though you have doubts, assure yourself that God is on your side, and in time you will understand why things happened the way they did.

My favorite passage in the Bible, which I have committed to memory and which I recite when I am in turmoil is Psalm 23:

The Lord is my shepherd, I shall not want.

He makes me to lie down in green pastures.
He leads me beside still waters.
He restores my soul.
He leads me in the path of

righteousness for his name's sake.

Though I walk in the valley of shadow of death, I fear no evil for You are with me.
Your rod and your staff they comfort me.

You prepare a table before me in the presence of my enemies.
My cup runs over.

Surely goodness and mercy will follow me for the rest of my life.

And I will dwell in the house of the Lord forever.

I would like to share with you my own prayer that has given me strength and peace every time I recite it:

You are my strength and my anchor,
Without You I am nothing.
Have mercy on me and hear my prayers.
Lead my life and be my guide.
Hold my hand and show me the way,
I trust in you completely,
May I do everything according to your will.

Prayer for myself	Prayer for my family	Prayer for someone else
_____	_____	_____
_____	_____	_____
_____	_____	_____
_____	_____	_____

QUIT THE BAD HABITS

Are you always doubting yourself? Do you keep on eating foods that your doctor said you should not eat? Do you find it difficult to quit smoking? Do you stay up late watching movies although you know you have to sleep a little earlier so you would not be late for school or work? Do you find yourself unable to get off social media or online games even when you know you should? Are you always thinking and predicting the worse before you even start doing anything? STOP! QUIT! Just end the bad habits.

Bad habits destroy us little by little, and this is what makes bad habits more dangerous. Because we think they are small things, we tend to overlook them. Take an inventory of your habits and see if any of these habits has a negative effect on your health and wellbeing. Then, when you start thinking about stopping it, listen carefully if there is a whisper coming from nowhere giving you all the reasons not to stop. Is it saying *"you don't have to stop it, it's different,"* or *"you don't have to stop it because it has not really adversely affected you,"* or *"you can stop next time?"* This is the result of us becoming so attached to our bad habits. It's about time we quash these thoughts. It is about time we take our power back over these bad habits. It is time to quit!

Think of a bad habit that you would like to quit. Reflect on the questions below:

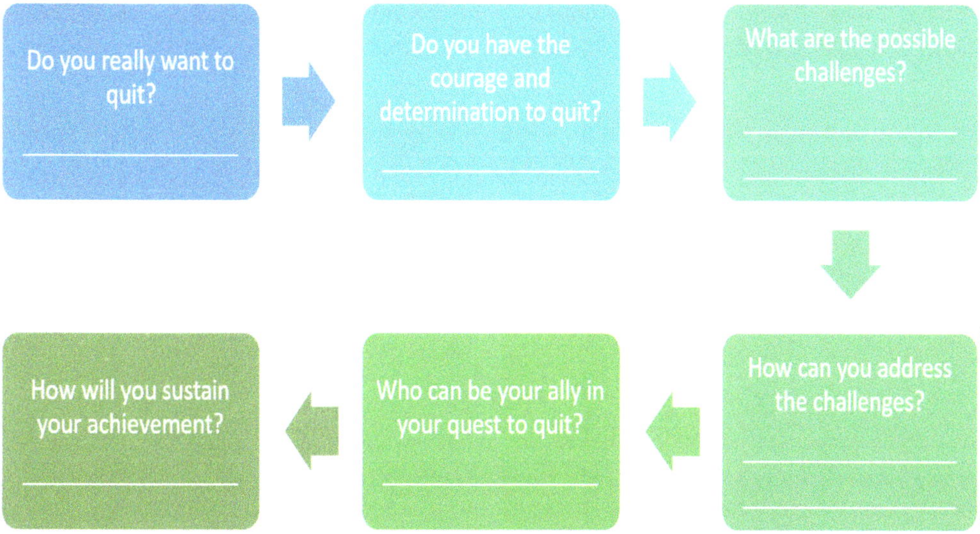

- Do you really want to quit? _____
- Do you have the courage and determination to quit? _____
- What are the possible challenges? _____
- How can you address the challenges? _____
- Who can be your ally in your quest to quit? _____
- How will you sustain your achievement? _____

RISE ABOVE YOUR PAIN

It is easier to say "rise above your pain" than to actually do it, and this is something that we should never ever say to anyone who is going through something painful in her/his life. No matter how much we think we understand other people's pain because we have been through something painful too, it will never be the same for any two people. The depth of the wound, the trauma that accompanies it, and the circumstances will always be different. No matter what the intention is, do not say these words to anyone in pain. Every person processes pain in different ways and we have to be respectful of this.

It is included here as a reflection point for you, when time has numbed some of your pain and you are already thinking of what to do with your life and how to move forward. When you have been in the dark for so long, and you can see that life is just passing you by, at some point you have to hold on to your strength, stand up, look pain in the eye, and say, I am bigger than you, I am above you, I will rise above you. Once you have made that decision, hold on to it, and move forward. The pain will still be there, but it will no longer immobilize you. Instead, it will propel you to fight and keep moving on. To be able to do this though you must have determination and strong will, and make the conscious effort to not let pain chain you into a life of despair and

agony. It is okay to cry when you feel the pain, but it should not define you or your life. Use it as a guide in making decisions but do not let it be the central force in your life. Let your pain give you a wider perspective about life and people.

Think of a painful experience that you would like to move on from, and then write a letter to yourself. Tell yourself about how you feel when you try to move on. Encourage yourself to look forward to a new tomorrow.

Dear _____,

_____
_____
_____
_____
_____
_____
_____
_____

Yours,

_____

SAY WHAT YOU NEED TO SAY

Have you ever been in a situation where right after an event, you will say to yourself, "I wish I said something," or "I wish I told them?" Regret comes after not saying what you wanted to say, especially words that we take for granted, or maybe words that we thought we would be able to say next time.

My husband died in a car accident in 2014. On his deathbed, when he was already declared brain dead, I was still talking to him, wishing and praying that somehow, he could still understand what I was saying. I wanted more time to tell him how much I love him, to just talk to him. But time was against us. He never woke up. There are nights when I still stare at the ceiling and wonder, while he was unconscious at the ICU, was there a chance he heard and understood the things I was telling him? Did he understand when I told him how grateful I was for all the things that he had done for me and our family? Did any of the words I said when he was unconscious mattered? I have always felt since he passed away that I should have said more *I love you* or more *I miss you* or even more, *how are you*.

Say what you have to say. Ask your family and friends, how they are. Tell the people who have done good things for you, "*thank you*." If needed, say, "*I am sorry*." And when people thank you, assure them they are welcome. Give yourself and the people around you time to talk. Give yourself the opportunity to say what you need to say.

What do you need to say? List them down and the names of people you would like to say these words to:

To	I would like to say

TAKE A STAND

I have read many times that those who stay in the middle of the road, those who cannot decide whether to go left or right, are the ones who are usually blown away, taken down, and crushed to the ground. How will taking a stand make a difference? Do you have to always be in an argument with anyone who carries a different set of beliefs? Do you always have to insist that what you know is right and should be followed? No. Taking a stand means standing up for your core values in any situation and never conceding your set of principles that make up your ethical and moral core. It also means knowing when to walk away from disagreements or conflicts and having the courage to actually walk away in peace. Taking a stand means knowing your position on issues and things and making decisions based on this. It could mean passionately fighting for what you believe in or walking away from distractions or petty things, or engaging in a diplomatic discussion, but always being guided by your core values. Taking a stand means living in this world peacefully,

putting your foot down when needed, and never compromising your values. When you know where you stand, you will always know where to go.

My Core Values

UNLOCK THAT PHONE AND CALL YOUR FRIENDS

We often see the expression "sister/brother from a different womb" or "siblings from different parents," or "friends who are like family." Lucky are we indeed to have friends that we consider as family. These are friends who supported us when we needed help, who cheered us when we were fighting for something, defended us when we were powerless, and offered a toast when we were victorious. When we are with our true friends, we speak the language of friendship, unbounded by time and distance, unmindful of diverging beliefs and opinion, and respectful of the differences.

In our lifetime, especially in this ever-changing world where we move from one job to another or live from one place to another, we will meet different kinds of friends – friends who will always be available for meet-ups, friends who will rarely show up but will show up at the exact moment when we need help the most, friends who will communicate with us only once in a blue moon but will give us the best advice and inspirational words, friends who will give us the ultimate support when we are at our lowest point but will eventually lose contact with, friends who will never forget any important event, and friends who will rarely talk but in their most special way will make us feel that we are important. Do not be affected by social media posts that say your true

friend will call you on your birthday, or your true friend will ask you how you are when there are typhoons, or any other qualifier for friendship. No one knows your friends better than you. Friends are God's way of saying here's a special angel for this particular time. If one day you wake up and texting or messaging a friend suddenly comes to mind, reach out to that friend. Do not set conditions before deciding to reach out. Do not wait for the right timing. Do not feel embarrassed that you will suddenly reach out after not being in contact for some time because friendship is not set upon some conditions or deadline. Friendship is a thread that binds your heart for life. Talk to your friends, listen to your friends, spend time with your friends. Keep your friendship locked in your hearts.

Choose something to do this month.

	Send an old fashioned birthday card to a friend.
	Send a thank you card via snail mail.
	Post an old photo with a friend who moved to another place.
	Give 3 friends a call.
	Send a message to a friend you have not seen for a long time
	Have coffee with a friend.
	Send a small token to an old colleague
	Do something special for a friend

VISUALIZE WHAT YOU WANT

Imagining what you want and then imprinting it in your mind is very, very powerful. When I was a little girl, I used to imagine how things would turn out because it inspires me and encourages me to work towards that picture in my mind. Without even knowing it, I was already visualizing – creating a vision of what I want to have or achieve. I was developing a vision for me and for my future. Visualizing your goals needs focus, dedication, clarity and constancy. You cannot stray from one thing to another because when you do that, you disperse the energy meant for your vision and you lose the strength of commitment and enthusiasm. Specifically, I remember when I was six years old, before going to bed every night, I imagined myself going up the stage, getting the ribbon for being an honor student, with my whole family watching me. That vision was so powerful because, unconsciously, it was pushing me to do better. It was making me more curious and more motivated. I started first grade as a nonreader but after two months, I was a fast reader, and indeed by the end of the school year, I was an honor student. My mother went up the stage with me to get my award.

Visualizing commands the forces of nature to make things work for you.

What are the words that trigger your mind to visualize for the future?

_____
_____
_____
_____
_____
_____
_____

Think of something that you really, really look forward to. Imagine that it is yours. Describe it below.

Welcome the Silver Lining

Things do not always work out the way we want them to be or expect them to be. Unexpected things happen, derailing our carefully laid-out plans. In this life, you are never really sure of anything. You could have been planning dinner with a friend you have not seen for many years but your car broke down so you could not go or you were planning a huge career change but a pandemic happened and the world stood still. If you are stuck in a situation you do not have control over or if you are faced with circumstances unfamiliar to you, what would you do? Assess your situation and find opportunities within your current limitations. Welcome the good things and opportunities that come with the unexpected – the silver lining. Even in our emotional experiences where we are confronted with challenging and difficult circumstances, let us always welcome the silver lining.

That silver lining is something we can hold on to – that little spark of hope, a seed of something good. It asks the question, are there opportunities to explore

other possibilities in my current situation? When you are in a dark hole, look for that silver lining, and when you find it embrace it and hold on to it. Let the silver lining bring a smile to your life.

REFLECTION: What is a difficult situation that you (or someone close to you) are going through right now. Considering the circumstances surrounding this situation, What silver lining can you find? What will you do with that silver lining?

_____
_____
_____
_____
_____
_____
_____
_____
_____
_____

'X' THE MEDIOCRITY; EXCEL IN ALL YOU DO

So many great talents have been wasted simply because they fell into the trap of mediocrity. Mediocrity is an evil lurking in the dark, stealing your passion, your determination, and destroying your hard work.

We can become so comfortable in what we are doing that even when there is an opportunity or a need to improve, we do the minimum acceptable standard. Worse, it could be below the minimum, hanging by just a thread on the minimum line. Watch out when you become too comfortable with anything or when everything seems too easy. Watch out when you can seem to finish everything that needs to be done without the need to exert effort. Check your work, check your process, and most importantly, check your attitude and feelings. Are you excited with the result of your work? Are you proud of your output? How you answer these questions will tell you how well you are doing in the excellence scale.

Let your work and your output be a source of your pride and honor. We must be vigilant against mediocrity. Do away with mediocrity and promote eXcellence!

I am taking these small steps to excellence!

I am taking these BIG steps to excellence!

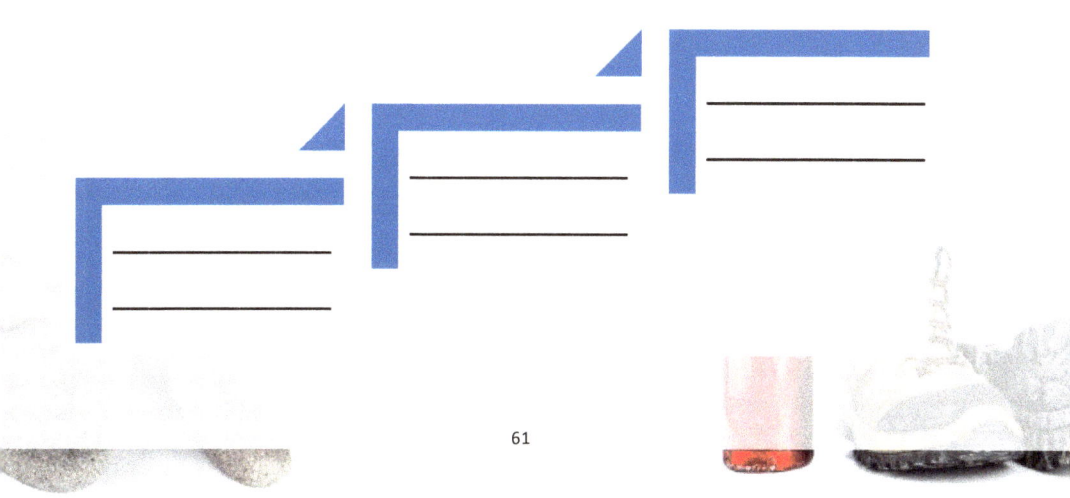

YOU TAKE CHARGE

No one else can make decisions for you except yourself, whether they are small decisions or big, life-changing decisions. You are in charge of your life and you decide how you move forward. When things are tough you are in charge of still moving forward. Even when you feel there is nothing else that can be done, you can decide to keep on fighting. When you feel so down that you think the world is about to crumble, you can choose to cry and then go on living or let the weight keep you down.

When things are good, you are in charge of keeping it that way. When things are going great you are in charge of planning to keep things great for the future.

When faced with making a difficult decision, there is a danger of being apathetic to the entire situation and decision-making process and just wait for things to unfold on its own. When you observe that this is happening to you, wake yourself up and remind yourself that you are in charge of your life and you have responsibilities in your community.

No matter what the circumstances are, you are in charge!

I am in charge of my life!

My name is _____. I am _____,
_____, and _____.

I am in charge of my life, and these are the decisions I am making right now:

_____
_____
_____
_____
_____
_____.

My name is _____, and I am in charge!

ZOOM TO WHERE YOU SHOULD BE, TO WHAT YOU WANT TO BE

And this is how it ends, with you moving wholeheartedly, purposefully and enthusiastically towards your goal – that place, that idea, that vision. It is not enough that you dream about it, talk about it, and prepare for it. You have to stand up, and work for it.

Enjoy this beautiful adventure called life. I wish you all the best on your journey! **May you have the opportunity to discover all the wonderful things that you can do!**

This is the image of where I want to be/what I want to be:

My reflection checklist:

	I read this book and reflected on its content.
	I find ways to enrich my spiritual life.
	I look after my health.
	I am supporting my community.
	I have focus and determination.
	I have a vision of what I want in the future.
	Happiness, faith, hope, and love are in my life.
	I am READY to take on challenges and move forward.
	I can visualize what I want.
	My dreams are alive in my heart.
	(Write your own)
	(Write your own)

EPILOGUE

The 20-kilometer walk was just the beginning of an exhausting and draining three years of living in utter poverty. After staying in a crowded house with limited food supply for a few days, we returned to our house, whatever is left of it. We stood motionless a few meters away from the rubble that used to be our house, half expecting the destruction but hoping against it. The house that was made of wood and bamboo was no match for the relentless volcanic ashfall. Parts of the house protruded here and there, creating a contrast against the backdrop of the white ashfall. There was nothing but ashfall around us. Trees gave in to the weight of the ashfall and were all buried too. The small creek dried up as it filled with ashfall. The place that used to be green with grass, trees and plants was an empty, desolate desert covered with overpowering sulfuric smell.

Hungry and tired, we started digging using our hands, hoping that we would chance upon cans of goods or anything that will be useful. We dug around the guava trees hoping some buried fruits will still be edible. Surprisingly, we did not feel despair nor fear. There was just the need to survive, and the feelings and emotions disappeared. We went with the flow of life – no more school for me and my siblings, no more work for my parents, falling in line for relief goods, eating sardines and noodles every single day, not taking a bath for days, and sleeping at night wondering when it will all end. I remember very clearly the day that I went to church where I was baptized. I was wearing the clothes that I had been in for several days, I sat at the back pew staring at the cross, asking God to keep us safe and to let us know what to do next. I sat there for a very long time. When I came out of the church, I proceeded to fall in line for the noodles and sardines.

A few days later, my mother's sister sent her husband to fetch us and take us to the province where they live. We left everything that we had, there was nothing much to leave anyway, and traveled for almost eight hours to start a new life. My father was left behind to try and see if he will still be able to work and be able to send us money. We had very little with us – a few set of clothes and the sack of school books. As the bus started to move, I looked back, one last time, disoriented and teary-eyed. How can life abruptly change – with dashed hopes and uncertain future. I did not have the chance to say goodbye to any of my friends or close relatives. Our departure from my birthplace was like the eruption of Mt. Pinatubo, sudden and unannounced.

In the province where we went, we were referred to as "*mga putok ng Pinatubo*" (spewed by Pinatubo). Help poured in when we arrived in the new province. We were given clothes to wear, rice, fruits, and other food items. Some even gave us money. The first few months were okay but as help dried up and our expenses and debts piled up – for food, for school, for childbirth, and for a lot of other things needed to live – I did laundry for other people where I had to pull out buckets of water from a deep well. I went to school with only one pair of school uniform and socks, and no food allowance. Every day, after school, I had to wash my school blouse, and with no electricity it would remain wet until the next day when I had to wear it again. Every morning, I walked going to school, traversing the side of the road where the sun shone the brightest so that my cold, wet blouse will be dry before I reach the school. The wet socks were more uncomfortable though, and every afternoon when I take it off, my feet will be wrinkled and smelly.

Sometimes, I cannot believe that we survived those three years with our spirit and dignity intact. I am still surprised by our resiliency, flexibility, hard work, and our ability to laugh, smile and stay happy when everything and the future was bleak. Those three years, I held on to God, hope, and my dreams. I have learned so many things from those three years, and when tragedies struck again – my father's death, and then my husband's accident and death – I leaned on the inner strength that was nourished on those three years from my youth.

Everything in this book came from my experiences, from the nuggets of wisdom that came with every heartbreak, tear and victory. I hope that this book will help remind you too of your own inner strength and resilience, and will motivate and inspire you to keep moving forward with hope and love in your heart and a genuine desire to help others.

ISBN: 978-621-96335-0-5

www.ingramcontent.com/pod-product-compliance
Lightning Source LLC
LaVergne TN
LVHW050137080526
838202LV00061B/6505